SPECIAL BOAT UNITS

by Michael Burgan

CAPSTONE BOOKS

an imprint of Capstone Press
Mankato, Minnesota

Capstone Books are published by Capstone Press
151 Good Counsel Drive, P. O. Box 669, Mankato, Minnesota 56002
http://www.capstone-press.com

Library of Congress Cataloging-in-Publication Data
Burgan, Michael.
    U.S. Navy special forces: special boat units/by Michael Burgan.
    p. cm.—(Warfare and weapons)
    Includes bibliographical references (p. 42) and index.
    Summary: Introduces the U.S. Navy's special boat units, their history, mission,
development, training, and equipment.
    ISBN 0-7368-0341-6
    1. United States. Navy. SEALs—Juvenile literature. 2. Special forces (Military
science)—United States—Juvenile literature. [1. United States. Navy. SEALs.
2. Special forces (Military science)] I. Title. II. Series.
VG87.B87 2000
359.9—dc21
                                                                 99-23156
                                                                      CIP

Editorial Credits
Blake Hoena, editor; Timothy Halldin, cover designer; Linda Clavel, illustrator:
    Heidi Schoof, photo researcher

Photo Credits
Corbis, 10, 12
Corbis/Leif Skoogfors, cover, 18
David Bohrer, 21
Defense Visual Information Center, 4, 7, 15, 22, 26, 28, 30, 32, 36, 38, 43, 44,
    47

**Special thanks to Naval Special Warfare Command Public Affairs for reviewing
this material, and to David Bohrer, Pulitzer Prize-winning photographer for the
Los Angeles Times, for providing an interior photo.**

Table of Contents

Chapter 1

Special Boat Units

During the late 1980s, Iran and Iraq were at war. This war threatened oil tankers in the region. These ships carried oil out of the Persian Gulf to the United States and other countries. The oil tankers were in danger from mines that Iranian sailors placed in the Persian Gulf. Mines are weapons that float in the water. They explode when ships sail into them.

The U.S. Navy sent Special Boat Unit (SBU) members to the Persian Gulf. These sailors helped protect the oil tankers. SBUs detected where the mines were and guided oil tankers safely past them. SBUs also patrolled

Mines float in the water and explode when ships sail into them.

the Persian Gulf. They attempted to stop Iranian sailors from placing any more mines in the water.

"Boat Guys"

Special Boat Unit members are specially trained members of the U.S. Navy. Their members operate some of the navy's small watercraft. These boats are built for special missions. SBUs often secretly transport soldiers safely to and from areas that larger ships cannot reach. SBU watercraft must be able to operate in shallow water. Their watercraft also must be able to move quickly on rivers and bays. SBU members often perform their duties in these types of waterways.

The navy currently has three SBUs. SBU-20 is based in Little Creek, Virginia. SBU-22 is based in Mississippi. SBU-12 is based in Coronado, California. Each SBU has about 200 sailors and 20 officers. Officers oversee sailors as they perform their duties. An SBU also may have as many as 30 boats.

SBU members operate the navy's small watercraft.

SBUs are part of Special Boat Squadrons. Squadrons consist of SBUs and Coastal Patrol ships. Special Boat Squadrons are commanded by the Naval Special Warfare Command.

The navy calls SBU members Special Warfare Combatant Craft Crewmen. But these sailors have their own nickname. They call themselves "Boat Guys."

SBU Operations

Special Boat Units are part of the navy's Special Operation Forces. They often perform clandestine operations. These missions are secret and may be dangerous. SBUs may support SEAL teams on these missions. SEAL stands for sea, air, and land. SEALs are highly trained members of the U.S. Navy. SEALs often sneak into enemy territory during their missions. SBUs may transport SEALs to mission sites.

SBUs also take part in missions that are not secret. They may patrol rivers or coastlines. SBU members on these missions watch for enemy ships or planes. SBU members also can sail their boats near larger ships that do not carry weapons. SBUs then can protect these larger ships if the ships are attacked.

SBUs also perform duties that are not related to war. SBUs sometimes help with counter-drug activities. They may stop ships that are suspected of carrying illegal drugs. SBU members then escort law enforcement officers aboard the ships. These officers then search for illegal drugs. SBUs also help during emergencies. For example, they can help rescue people during floods. SBUs use their boats to carry these people to safety.

Stars: The three stars represent three campaigns SBUs were involved in during the Vietnam War; these were the Market Time, Game Warden, and Sea Lords campaigns.

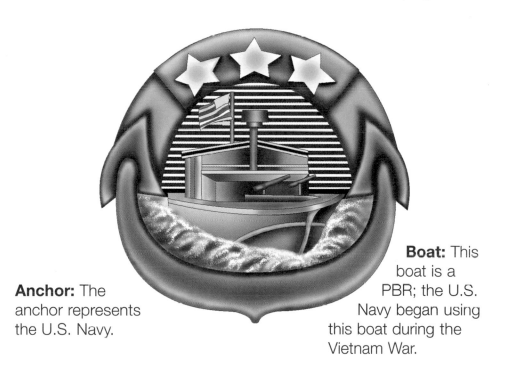

Anchor: The anchor represents the U.S. Navy.

Boat: This boat is a PBR; the U.S. Navy began using this boat during the Vietnam War.

Chapter 2

History of SBUs

The U.S. Navy fought battles on both the Atlantic and Pacific Oceans during World War II (1939–1945). The navy had many large ships. But these ships could not get close to shore. Instead, the navy used amphibious landing craft. These craft carried soldiers from the larger ships to the shore. But these craft were not designed to attack other ships.

The navy developed Patrol Torpedo (PT) boats. PT boats carried two to four torpedoes. These missiles speed through the water toward enemy ships. PT boats could sail in oceans. They also could sail in shallow waters close to shore. The navy used these boats to attack enemy vessels. They also were used to protect

Amphibious landing craft carried soldiers to shore during World War II.

PT boats used torpedoes to attack enemy vessels.

amphibious landing craft. PT boat crews
performed duties similar to those of today's
Special Boat Units.

Vietnam

In the 1960s, the United States began to send
troops to fight in the Vietnam War (1954–1975).
Much of this fighting was riverine. Many battles
took place on or near rivers. The navy needed
boats that could patrol these waters. The navy
used amphibious landing craft from World

War II for this purpose. They added new guns to these craft. But the craft were too slow to be effective.

The navy then designed boats especially for riverine combat. One such boat was the Patrol Boat, Riverine (PBR). These boats could operate in shallow water. They also moved quickly in narrow waterways. The navy specially trained sailors to run these boats. Part of their duties were to bring Navy SEALs to mission sites. These new boats and their sailors formed the first Special Boat Units.

During the Vietnam War, SBUs dropped off SEALs in enemy territory. SBU members then waited while the SEALs performed their missions. SBUs also helped defend the SEALs if they were attacked.

At first, the navy called SBUs Mobile Support Teams and Coastal River Divisions. These units were part of the navy nicknamed the "Brown Water Navy." The Brown Water Navy consisted of boats built to work in shallow waters such as rivers. The water in Vietnamese rivers often was muddy and looked brown. The sailors on these boats also had their own nickname. They called themselves "River Rats."

Other Missions

Special Boat Unit members and SEALs still work closely together. Members of SBU-12 and SBU-20 work mainly with SEAL teams. Members of SBU-22 train for riverine warfare.

The best-known SBU missions involve SEALs and other Special Operations Forces. In 1983, SBU-20 transported SEALs to a Caribbean island called Grenada. The U.S. government sent troops there to protect U.S. medical students. The U.S government believed the students were threatened by rebels. These people had overthrown the elected Grenadian government. SEALs led the invasion of the island. SBU members helped rescue the medical students.

SBUs were involved in many other missions. In 1989, U.S. forces invaded Panama during Operation Just Cause. U.S. military forces were sent to Panama to capture General Manuel Noriega. Noriega was using his

SBU members help protect larger ships.

military force to keep the elected government out of power. SBU members transported troops during this operation.

During the Gulf War (1991), SBUs brought SEALs to mission sites in Kuwait. In 1994, the U.S. military sent troops to the African nation of Somalia. These troops acted as a police force. They helped protect the starving citizens of this country and supply these people with food. SBU-20 performed 54 combat missions there.

Mission

Operation: Earnest Will

Date: 1987

Location: Persian Gulf

Situation: Iraq and Iran were at war. The warring countries had placed mines in the gulf's waters. These mines endangered oil tankers sailing in the Persian Gulf.

SBU: The U.S. military sent SBU members to the Persian Gulf. They detected where the mines were in the water. The SBU members then guided oil tankers safely past the mines. SBU members also patrolled the Persian Gulf. They tried to stop Iranian sailors from placing more mines in the water.

Ajar: U.S. military forces spotted an Iranian ship dropping mines in the water. This ship was called the Ajar. U.S. helicopters attacked the ship. SBU boats then carried SEALs to the Ajar. The SEALs boarded the Ajar and captured the surviving Iranian sailors on board.

Chapter 3

Becoming an SBU Sailor

Sailors volunteer to join Special Boat Units. They are members of the U.S. Navy who offer to serve in these units. But only men can join SBUs. Congressional law does not allow women to enter combat specialties. These jobs may involve duties that are performed while under direct fire from enemy forces.

Not everyone who volunteers becomes an SBU member. First, these volunteers must pass certain tests. The most important is a physical fitness test. It is the same test navy SEALs must pass. The sailors must be able to swim 500 yards (457 meters) in 12.5 minutes. They

The members of SBUs volunteer for special training.

then do 42 push-ups in two minutes. They follow that with 50 sit-ups and at least eight pull-ups. The last part of the fitness test is a 1.5-mile (2.4-kilometer) run.

SWCC Course

Trainees who pass all the physical tests take a special course for Special Boat Unit Trainees. This course is called the Special Warfare Combatant Crewman (SWCC) Course. Most of the course is taught at the Navy Amphibious Base in Coronado, California. Navy SEALs also train there.

The SEAL training course is known for being very difficult. More than half of the sailors who start it do not finish. SBU training is almost as difficult. It lasts for nine weeks. About 25 percent of the trainees who start the SWCC Course do not finish.

The SWCC Course involves a great deal of daily exercise. Trainees run, do push-ups, and swim. Trainees often swim wearing their uniform.

SBU trainees spend many hours studying in classrooms.

Trainees learn how to row small rubber boats called Zodiacs. SBUs often use these boats during missions.

Trainees also study in the classroom. They learn about the different watercraft SBUs use. Each trainee must learn how to perform all of the duties aboard each type of boat. Trainees also must learn to read naval charts and maps.

SBU members train using weapons more than most navy sailors.

It is important that trainees learn all the duties aboard each SBU watercraft. An SBU member could get hurt during a mission. Someone else on his boat must be able to take over his job. Most navy members only train to do just one duty aboard a ship.

Training for Combat
After classroom training, trainees go to sea. They spend as many as 16 hours a day on

boats. Trainees learn how to use boats to patrol rivers and ocean coasts.

Special Boat Unit trainees spend their last two weeks of training on San Clemente Island. This island is off California's coast. Trainees learn how to use different weapons there. These include rifles, pistols, and machine guns. SBU trainees train with weapons more than most navy sailors.

SBU trainees also learn what to do if their boats are destroyed. They then might have to swim ashore. They would have to stay hidden if they were in enemy territory. Trainees learn how to avoid being captured by enemy forces.

On the Job

Trainees who complete the SWCC Course are assigned to a Special Boat Unit. But they still continue to train. SBU members must be ready for duty at all times. An SBU might be sent anywhere in the world to fight with Special Operation Forces. SBUs can be ready for a mission within 48 hours.

SBUs must be prepared for every mission. SBU members load their boats and equipment on large planes. SBU members make sure they have enough water, food, and gas for their missions. They make sure they have bullets for their guns. They also make sure all their equipment works properly.

Each SBU boat has an officer in charge (OIC). The OICs may meet with SEALs to plan missions. During these missions with SEALs, SBU members often must transport SEALs to their mission sites. SBU members then patrol or perform other duties as they wait for the SEALs to complete their missions. SBUs pick up the SEALs when their missions are completed. OICs decide the best ways to perform these tasks.

SEALs sometimes come under attack. SBU members must help defend them. The SBUs speed away once the SEALs are aboard the boats. This is the most dangerous part of SBU members' duties.

Military Terms

Boat Guys – a nickname for today's SBU sailors

Brown Water Navy – a term used for naval units trained for riverine use

CRRC – Compact Rubber Raiding Craft; the CRRC is also called a Zodiac.

Hooyah – a word spoken when a person agrees with what someone else is saying

HSB – High Speed Boat

MATC – Mini-Armored Troop Carrier

OIC – Officer in Charge

PBL – Patrol Boat, Light

PBR – Patrol Boat, Riverine

PT – Patrol Boat

River Rats – a nickname for SBU sailors during the Vietnam War

SBU – Special Boat Unit

SOC – Special Operations Craft

SWCC Course – Special Warfare Combatant Crewman Course

Chapter 4

Boats of Many Sizes

The most important tools for Special Boat Units are their watercraft. These boats come in many sizes. They may carry machine guns and other weapons. The SBUs use different boats for different types of missions. SBUs decide which boats to use for a mission based on their size and speed.

Mark V Special Operations Craft

The Mark V Special Operations Craft (SOC) is the newest and fastest watercraft used by Special Boat Units. A Mark V can reach speeds of nearly 60 miles (97 kilometers) per hour. This boat is 82 feet (25 meters) long. It

SBUs use many types of watercraft.

The Mark V is one of the navy's newest special operations craft.

can carry as many as 16 SEALs or other special operations troops.

Enemy troops often use radar to locate boats. This electronic system uses radio waves to locate objects that are far away. But the Mark V is hard to see with radar because of its design. This helps the Mark V crew perform missions in secret.

The Mark V has five weapon placements. SBU members can mount machine guns and grenade launchers in each of these spots. The Mark V also can carry Stinger missiles. SBU members can fire these missiles at aircraft.

High Speed Boat

The High Speed Boat (HSB) is another fast watercraft. But it has fewer weapon placements than the Mark V. SBU members use HSBs when there is little danger of an enemy spotting them. HSBs are similar to speedboats used by civilians outside of the military.

SBUs used HSBs during the Gulf War. SBUs often used these boats to carry SEALs to shore in enemy territory. The SEALs then planted bombs and retreated aboard the boats.

Patrol Boats

Over the years, SBUs used different types of patrol boats. The Patrol Boat, Riverine (PBR) was one of the first such boats built. The navy had hundreds of these boats built during the Vietnam War. PBRs were 31 feet (9.4 meters)

long. SBU members used these boats mainly on rivers. PBRs also carried machine guns and a small cannon called a mortar.

Most boats use propellers to move through water. These spinning metal blades may extend several feet below the water's surface. Propellers might hit the bottom of shallow waterways. A PBR's engine shoots out jets of water to move the boat forward. The PBR's jets are closer to the water's surface. This allows PBRs to travel in much more shallow water than watercraft with propellers.

The navy also built patrol boats to use in deeper waters. The Mark III is almost twice as long as the PBR. It also carries more weapons. The Mark IV is similar to the Mark III. But the Mark IV has larger engines and can travel faster than the Mark III.

Another patrol boat is the Patrol Boat, Light (PBL). The PBL is 25 feet (7.6 meters) long and can reach speeds of more than 40 miles (64 kilometers) per hour. It carries two

Many SBU watercraft are designed for patrolling various types of waterways.

machine guns. SBUs use PBLs to scout waterways before an attack.

Rigid-Hull Inflatable Boat

SBUs usually use the Rigid-Hull Inflatable Boat (RIB) to bring SEALs to mission sites. The bottom half of the boat is made out of fiberglass. This light, strong material is made from glass fibers. The upper half of the RIB has a thick cloth covering. The cloth is filled with air. This makes the boat float. This cloth also is very strong. It does not tear easily.

The RIB comes in three sizes. It can be 24 feet (7 meters), 30 feet (9 meters), or 36 feet (11 meters) long. The 24-foot RIB carries four SEALs. The two larger RIBs carry as many as eight SEALs. The 36-foot model can reach speeds of more than 50 miles (80 kilometers) per hour.

Like PBRs, RIBs use jets for power. They can operate in water that is just a few feet deep. They also can sail through high waves.

SBUs use the RIB to transport SEALs to mission sites.

Mini-Armored Troop Carrier

The U.S. Marines used the Mini-Armored Troop Carrier (MATC). But SBUs also decided to use this craft to transport Special Operations troops. It is 36 feet (11 meters) long. MATCs have machine guns and grenade launchers. They can travel more than 30 miles (48 kilometers) per hour in water just 18 inches (46 centimeters) deep. The MATC's engine uses water jets.

Important Dates

1939 – World War II begins; U.S. Navy develops PT boats.

1950 – Korean War begins

1954 – Vietnam War begins

1966 – PBRs used in Vietnam

1975 – Mark III patrol boat first used

1983 – Operation Urgent Fury; SBUs transport SEAL teams during U.S. invasion of Grenada.

1986 – Mark IV patrol boat first used

1987 – Operation Earnest Will; U.S. Navy assigns SBU members to protect oil tankers in Persian Gulf.

1989 – Operation Just Cause; U.S. forces invade Panama.

1990s – SBUs begin using the RIB

1990 – Operation Desert Storm; SBUs transport SEALs to mission sites.

1994 – Operation Restore Hope; SBUs perform more than 50 missions in Somalia, Africa.

1995 – SBUs begin using the Mark V Special Operations Craft

Chapter 5

The Future

Special Boat Units will continue to sail their small, fast craft in the future. They sometimes will transport SEALs to mission sites. They also will work by themselves. SBUs will use their skills to patrol and reach shallow waterways that larger ships cannot reach.

Training and Humanitarian Missions
SBUs members also help train sailors from other countries. They have worked with sailors from countries in the Middle East and Central America. They also help train sailors from Asia and Europe. SBU members teach these sailors to use small watercraft.

SBUs also perform humanitarian missions. The U.S. government often helps other

Small watercraft are an important part of the navy's fleet.

nations after wars. It also may provide aid to other countries after natural disasters such as floods or hurricanes. U.S. troops may be sent to help provide people with food, water, and housing. SBUs can transport humanitarian supplies by boat. They also can carry people to safe areas during floods.

Small boats are important to the U.S. Navy. But the boats need specially trained sailors on board. "Boat Guys" are always prepared to perform their missions. They will continue to support SEALs and other Special Operations troops in the future.

The navy needs sailors specially trained to sail its small watercraft.

Words to Know

amphibious (am-FIB-ee-us)—able to work on both land and water

clandestine operations (KLAN-des-tuhn op-uh-RAY-shuhns)—secret missions

fiberglass (FYE-bur-glass)—a strong, light material made from glass fibers

grenade (gruh-NADE)—a small bomb; some types of this explosive device can be thrown by soldiers and other types can be fired from a grenade launcher.

humanitarian mission (hyoo-man-uh-TER-ee-uhn MISH-uhn)—a mission that helps people in need

insignia (in-SIG-nee-ah)—a pin worn by members of a group; the pin shows that all the members belong to the same group.

mine (MINE)—an explosive device that floats in the water

mortar (MOR-tur)—a small cannon

propeller (pruh-PEL-ur)—a set of spinning metal blades that move a boat through water

rebel (REB-uhl)—a person who is against an elected government

riverine (RI-vur-een)—relating to activity on or near a river

Special Operations (SPESII-uhl op-uh-RAY-shuhns)—military missions using highly trained troops

squadron (SKWAHD-ruhn)—a naval unit of two or more divisions

torpedo (tor-PEE-doh)—a missile that travels under water to hit ships or submarines

To Learn More

Bohrer, David. *America's Special Forces.* Osceola, Wis.: MBI Publishing Company, 1998.

Green, Michael. *River Patrol Boats.* Land and Sea. Mankato, Minn.: Capstone Books, 1999.

Halberstadt, Hans. *U.S. Navy SEALs in Action.* Osceola, Wis.: Motorbooks International, 1995.

Streissguth, Tom. *U.S. Navy SEALs.* Serving Your Country. Minneapolis: Capstone Press, 1996.

Stubblefield, Gary and Hans Halberstadt. *Inside the U.S. Navy SEALs.* Osceola, Wis.: Motorbooks International, 1995.

Useful Addresses

Naval Special Warfare Center
Naval Amphibious Base
San Diego, CA 92118

UDT SEAL Museum
3300 N A1A North Hutchinson Island
Fort Pierce, FL 34949

Internet Sites

Naval Special Warfare Command
http://www.navsoc.navy.mil

Navy SEALs
http://www.chinfo.navy.mil/navpalib/factfile/
    personnel/seals/seals.html

Special Boat Unit 11 Memorial Site
http://geocities.com/Pentagon/3204/sbu11.htm

Special Boat Units
http://www.blarg.net/~whitet/sbu.htm

U.S. Navy
http://www.navy.mil

U.S. Special Boat Units
http://www.specialforces.net/navy/SBU/
    default.htm

Index